Table of Contents

T0015874

Chapter 1

HISTORY OF JEWELRY

Jewelry is not a new accessory. Many people have enjoyed showing off their jewelry throughout history. People wear jewelry to dress up their outfits, to represent their culture, and for many other reasons.

In ancient times, people found natural materials in their environment to make jewelry and other types of accessories. The oldest found pieces of jewelry were beads made of shells one hundred thousand years ago.

A necklace of fish bones from twenty-five thousand years ago has also been discovered. People have been making jewelry from animal parts such as shells, teeth, bones, and bird feathers, and materials such as crystals, gemstones, and pearls for thousands of years.

THESE PIECES OF JEWELRY WERE FOUND IN SPAIN AND PROBABLY MADE SOMETIME BETWEEN 2300–700 BCE.

Pearls have been found in oysters living up to 125 feet (40 m) deep in the ocean.

Style and Stones

Jewelry, like most things that have been around for ages, has taken on different meanings. Jewelry has been symbols of love, money, country, and culture.

The more creative a jeweler is, the more interesting the pieces become. From precious stones found deep in the ocean to friendship bracelets traded between the best of friends, jewelry has quite a reputation and continues to rule the fashion world.

That's a Fact!

For centuries, jewelry made out of insects has played an important role in many cultures. Ancient Egyptians wore scarab beetle amulets. The scarab beetle represented Re, the Egyptian god of the sun. In modern times, South American Indigenous groups wear living insects as live jewelry. Beetles and cockroaches are the most common insects to be worn this way. Wearing live insects is an important part of their culture.

The cover of this Egyptian container looks like a scarab beetle.

Chapter 2

MODERN JEWELRY TRENDS

Young people are always looking for ways to express themselves. One way is through jewelry. They make bold choices and pick items that reflect the world around them, making them major jewelry trendsetters.

Nameplate necklaces, huge hoop earrings, and updated vintage looks are raging through young Hollywood.

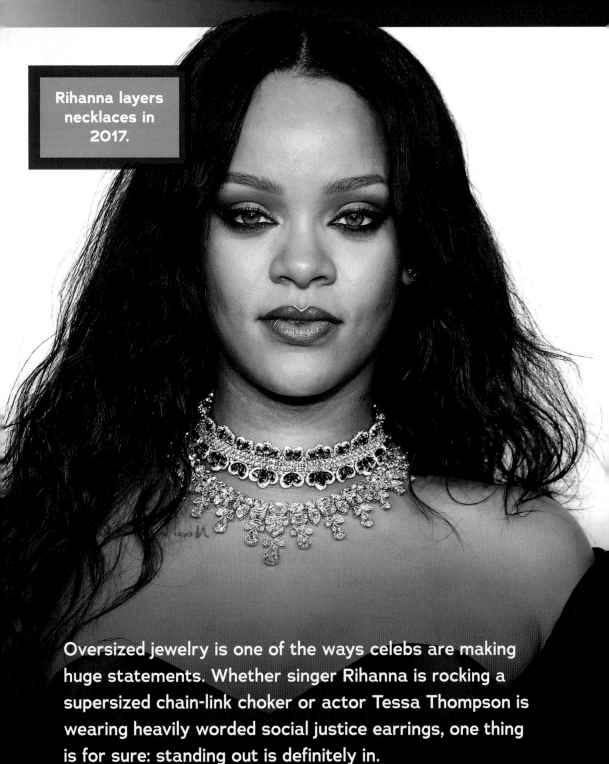

Oversized jewelry is one of the ways celebs are making huge statements. Whether singer Rihanna is rocking a supersized chain-link choker or actor Tessa Thompson is wearing heavily worded social justice earrings, one thing is for sure: standing out is definitely in.

Household metal objects can be made into bold jewelry choices. Key necklaces, padlock bracelets, and

safety pin earrings are being glammed up by celebs like Taylor Swift and Zendaya. They transform a simple jeans-and-T-shirt look into edgy rocker glam.

Mix and Match

Pearls are in! Young celebs like Gigi Hadid and Amandla Stenberg are updating the pearl look into chunky, funky jewelry. By layering glass beads and metallic chains over preppy pearls, any teen will be ready for a close-up.

Hadid pairs pearls with a metallic outfit.

Earrings are another fun way for fashion fans to express themselves. Teens are going bare in one ear and flashy in the other. By rocking this asymmetrical look, celebs like Bella Hadid turn heads on the red carpet. And hoop earrings, like the ones dangling from Selena Gomez's and Beyoncé's ears, will never go out of style.

Gomez wows with her statement hoop earrings in 2019.

Singer Katy Perry has been wearing fruit jewelry for years. Kids everywhere are trying on strawberry chokers and dangling lemons and cherries from their ears. These fun accessories come in plastic or metal.

Fruit-inspired jewelry adds a fun flair to any look.

Singer Lil Nas X almost always wears his signature earring cross in his left ear. Actor and singer Harry Styles likes to wear his necklace that spells out the word *golden* to reflect how he feels driving down the coast.

Lil Nas X wears an earring and rings to reflect his style in 2020.

Jewelry used to be all about looking fabulous. But things are changing. These days, many people are into buying items for multiple purposes. Some people walk through town with their cell phones hanging from their fingertips. Their cell phone cases come with a hidden finger holder. This piece of metal not only helps you hold onto your phone but also doubles as a fancy finger accessory.

Finger holders on phone cases come in a variety colors and options for bling.

Style Icon

JoJo Siwa loves to dance, sing, and wear her signature hair bows. She also has her own jewelry line. Siwa appeared in two seasons of the reality show *Dance Moms*. Her fun personality and cute style eventually led to contracts with Nickelodeon, an international singing and dancing tour called D.R.E.A.M., and one of the most successful YouTube channels for kids. Siwa's iconic hair bows *and* bow-shaped earrings and necklaces are sold at many stores.

Siwa rocks her bow-shaped earrings in 2017.

15

Chapter 3

CREATING YOUR LOOK

Stocking a beginner's jewelry box and accessories can be easy, fun, and affordable. It's all about who you are.

You can never go wrong by investing in a delicate necklace. It can clean up a casual look and simmer down a fierce outfit. For special occasions, swapping out the go-to necklace for a chunky choker can be fun.

The chunky choker is a celebrity statement necklace. Rihanna likes to sport a 1-inch-thick (2.5 cm) gold choker or chain, and so do Usher, Kim Kardashian, Jennifer Lopez, French Montana, and other stars.

Chains elevate any look. This Cuban link chain is one of the most popular chain styles.

Simple to Edgy

A simple pair of stud earrings are essential to everyone's jewelry stash. A pair of studs can take casual to elegant or balance out a dramatic makeup pairing. But for special occasions, go for a pair of hoops or something bigger and brighter. If you're wearing dramatic earrings, pair them with a simple outfit. A well-fitted, plain T-shirt with a pair of jeans is a classic look that always pairs well with dramatic earrings.

Stud earrings can soften a look.

For must-have rings, a delicate band checks in at number one. It pairs with everything and adds a soft touch to your look. Jaden Smith likes wearing one or more silver bands on his fingers. You can't go wrong with simplicity. Rings are also a great way to show off your individuality. Young celebs like Bad Bunny stack their fingers with colorful or uniquely shaped rings to keep things interesting.

Thick, silver bands are edgy.

Watches can add sophistication and class to an outfit. They're often more about style than telling the time. Try pairing a cute watch with stacks of bracelets.

Layering bracelets with a wristwatch can help you incorporate colors and textures.

That's a Fact!

Diamond jewelry is popular, but mining for diamonds is bad for the environment. In the 1950s, scientists in labs learned how to grow gems that look identical to real diamonds. The cubic zirconia became wildly popular because it's environmentally friendly, it's affordable, and unless you're a diamond expert with a microscope, it looks like the real thing.

Experts look at a stone's edges to see if it is a diamond or cubic zirconia. Since diamonds are very hard, if the stone looks soft or worn, it is likely cubic zirconia.

No die-hard rules exist about adding accessories to pump up a great look. But if you're going for the dramatic necklace, maybe save the dramatic earrings for next time. Or maybe you're going to an event perfect for both. You're ultimately in charge of how you want to style your jewelry. No one has to be locked into a certain style. You can have as much fun as you want expressing yourself.

Mix and match styles to create your own look.

Chapter 4

BECOME A JEWELER

Creating custom jewelry is one of the easiest ways to show off personal style. Most craft stores have everything you need to make your own jewelry or accessorize your clothes—beads, wire, pliers, glue, and even instruction manuals.

The jewelry-making possibilities can be endless. Many techniques and materials are used to make jewelry. Practice one type of jewelry making first before branching out to other types.

YOU MIGHT START MAKING JEWELRY BY FOCUSING ON YOUR FAVORITE TYPE, SUCH AS NECKLACES.

You can create your own jewelry with beads, rubber bands, or whatever you want.

Make a Statement

Beaded bracelets can be fun and easy pieces of jewelry to make. Using stretchy jewelry string and assorted letter beads, you can string your bestie's name together in no time to make a fabulous friendship bracelet. You can wear just one bracelet on your wrist to show off your best friend, or you can rock many bracelets at once to show off all your favorite friends. Remember to double knot the stretchy string when you're done making it so that it doesn't loosen and beads don't scatter everywhere.

BY MAKING YOUR OWN BRACELETS, YOU CAN SHOW OFF YOUR STYLE AND CREATIVITY.

▼

Are you wondering what to do with all those leftover letters? You can share your interests with the world. Spell out your favorite sport, color, or team!

Many kids are into social justice. They like to let everyone know where they stand on important issues like human rights and the environment.

String together words like *justice* or *equality.* If you really want to get your message across, assemble phrases like Black Lives Matter, LGBTQIA+, Quality Health Care, and Save Our Environment onto your stretchy string. You can also color-code your social justice bracelets to represent a movement or group. For example, use green letters for your Save Our Environment bracelet, black and brown letters for Black Lives Matter, and all the colors in the rainbow for LGBTQIA+.

Black Lives Matter is easy to read on this bracelet. Gray beads separate the words.

Bracelets are a great way to express yourself!

Some kids like to wear pins on their jackets or backpacks, but these tiny enamel pieces can be costly. So bracelets are a great alternative.

Stack your wrist with bracelets showing several topics that you care about. This is a fun way to express your interests. It's also a positive, uplifting reminder of the things you love that you can look at throughout your day!

Jewelry Hack

You can make your own fabric bracelets by repurposing T-shirts you no longer wear into a brand-new fabric. With a parent's or guardian's permission, use a pair of scissors to cut one long strip out of a colorful T-shirt. Cut the strip in half and tie the ends together to complete the bracelet. If you want a cool design, make several half cuts into the strip to make a frayed fabric bracelet. If you're feeling crafty, cut strips from three different-colored T-shirts and braid the strips together for a cute braided-fabric bracelet.

Glossary

accessory: something added to an outfit such as scarves, bracelets, and rings

amulet: a small wearable object that some believe protects the wearer from bad things

asymmetrical: not the same on both sides

culture: the beliefs or customs of a group of people

custom jewelry: personalized jewelry

environment: the natural world

friendship bracelet: a bracelet made of string given to another as a symbol of friendship

gemstone: a special stone often used in jewelry

repurpose: to use something for a different purpose

stud: a small piece of jewelry that is worn through the earlobe, nose, or another part of the body

vintage: something that is not new but that is valued because of its condition, design, or other quality